OWN YOUR
PHENOMENAL
SELF

A GUIDE ON CHARACTER,
SUCCESS, & LEADERSHIP

D0062253

RITA P. MITCHELL

DEDICATION

To young women everywhere who
are ambitious, highly motivated, and
who want to do good in the world:
You have enough, you are enough,
You have been and always will be
PHENOMENAL,
AND...the best is yet to come!

ISBN: 978-1-7329102-0-1 (Paperback)
ISBN: 978-1-7329102-1-8 (Ebook)

Library of Congress Control Number: 2018966105

Front cover image: from iStockphoto 2018; uzenzen, original artist
Cover design: Chris Ward
Interior design: Doug Cordes

Printed in the United States of America.
First printing edition 2019.

www.RitaPMitchell.com

PRAISE FOR
OWN YOUR PHENOMENAL SELF

"Rita Mitchell's authentic voice of wisdom comes from the experiences of a successful life and career. Spend ninety minutes with this book and you will be ready to own your power."

> — **LINDA PEEK SCHACHT,** former Vice President, The Coca-Cola Company, and Founding Director, Lipscomb University Nelson and Sue Andrews Institute for Civic Leadership

"Rita P. Mitchell's *Own Your Phenomenal Self* provides a message of empowerment that is heartfelt and essential reading. She does not sugarcoat the message but does make it authentic and relevant. I have served in senior leadership roles in government, private equity owned and publicly traded for-profit corporations, and nonprofits. I find Rita's message universally true for all sectors."

> —**SHARON K. ROBERSON,** President & CEO, YWCA Nashville & Middle Tennessee

"Rita Mitchell illuminates the reality of 'owning it' in her intensely personal, honest, and insightful book, *Own Your Phenomenal Self*. By sharing lessons she has lived and learned, she invites us all to look inward at what holds us back and offers us important takeaways and heartfelt advice. If you feel 'stuck' in your career or are struggling to find that 'next level' of success, this book will help you confront your internal obstacles, sharpen your focus, and achieve your potential. Thank you Rita!"

> — **SARA J. FINLEY,** Principal, Threshold Corporate Consulting, and former General Counsel, CVS Caremark Corporation

"When navigating winding paths or dark streets, we all want to follow someone who has a bright flashlight—Rita Mitchell not only shines her light for those coming behind her, but she settles into a comfy bench with a great vista in front of her and invites you to sit down and consider the journey ahead. Fabulous."

> — **TRISH CRIST,** CEO, Nashville Education, Community, and Arts Television (NECAT)

"I wish I could have had access to this book many years ago. It would have saved me from a lot of heartache. Rita's advice is tried and true!"

> — **PATRICIA PIERCE,** National Women's History Project Board of Directors, Retired Administrator, Vanderbilt University, Former Commissioner, Tennessee Human Rights Commission

"Where was a book like this when I was twenty-five? Where was a woman like Rita Mitchell in my life and career path when I was twenty-five? The ability to give a hand up and a nudge forward to a woman from a woman—especially when we think we have to be anything but who we really are to succeed—could've changed the paths for so many women who went at it alone when we were twenty-five. I've known Rita for over ten years, and one night when a group of us had dinner together and she told me her story, I knew I wanted more of her, her wisdom, her authenticity, and her "bad-assness" around me. This book will motivate and guide many women who were like me twenty-five years ago! And hopefully, with the guiding points at the end of each chapter, it will give that woman a clear guide on how to embrace their Phenomenal Selves and point their internal compass to True North."

> — **CHRISTIE WILSON,** President and Broker, The Wilson Group Real Estate Services

"In a world of corporate landscapes often rife with hidden agendas, power plays, and ambiguity of ethics—particularly for ambitious and talented women—Rita P. Mitchell offers an alternative response and course of action. *Own Your Phenomenal Self* is much more than a good book. Rita's personal stories can—and, in my opinion, should—be every professional woman's GPS for navigating pitfalls, setbacks, boobytraps, and—on occasion—corporate idiocy with the fuel of integrity, engine of tenacity, tires of kindness, auto body of committed excellence, and an individually unique key of personal purpose. This book changed me for the better. I urge you to read and risk the same."

— **GENIE JAMES,** internationally-recognized author and speaker and CEO of GJ Enterprises

"*Own Your Phenomenal Self* is an excellent book for women in any stage of their career and particularly for those who are interested in maximizing the gifts and talents they've been given. It is a thoughtful combination of real-life experiences, wisdom, and practical tips. It is easy to read yet provides the reader with insight and thought-provoking activities to enhance their lives and careers. This will be a valuable resource that spans decades."

— **DEBRA BOBLITT,** former Senior Vice President of the Southeastern Market of State Farm Insurance

"*Own Your Phenomenal Self* is chock-full of gems of wisdom for corporate/professional survival, success, and self-actualization on the journey to authentic self. A quick read and reference guide, Rita Mitchell's personal journey is inspirational and provides practical advice that can be applied in challenging situations. It should be the go-to handbook on the desk of aspiring professionals and leaders."

— **D. BILLYE SANDERS,** Attorney-at-Law

"Rita Mitchell has written a very relevant and thoughtful book that is based on her life's experience as an African American and a woman navigating the business world starting in the '70s through present day. Her book is an inspiring and practical guide for any woman (or man) who wants to be successful and make the most of their talent. Additionally, it could be a significant help for anyone who has hit a roadblock and needs to kick-start their career. Her book is a big gift in a small package."

— **LADY BIRD,** retired Corporate Officer and Government Executive

"*Own Your Phenomenal Self* is a book that is both meaningful and thought-provoking. It is full of excellent guidance for young women (and men) who are striving to make their mark in the business world. What I found particularly useful was Rita's advice about the importance of connecting. My favorite passage is, 'You must learn to sincerely connect with people and become a master of the connect. And because people connect with those they like, know, and trust, it follows that you must be likable, you must know and be known to people on a personal level, and you must create a level of trust, which can only happen when you yourself are trustworthy.'"

— **LEIGH WALTON,** Member, Bass, Berry & Sims

"Wow! What a powerful, motivating and inspiring read! If this does not get young (and seasoned) women to walk in their purpose I am not sure what will. I am not sure how I can relive my career but I sure can pass on Rita's story to many young women that I know in the middle of their careers. I am confident that this will be a guide and an inspiration to so many."

— **ROXIANNE BETHUNE,** Diversity Business Consultant

"Mitchell's authentic account of professional realities with clear-cut guidance for responding constructively is refreshingly sincere. Invaluable perspective from a successful leader that I highly recommend to professionals and their mentors alike."

— **EVETTE WHITE,** CEO, Executive Selection

"This book was very instrumental in providing the clarity I needed to regain control over my career to return to the driver's seat. The examples and analogies drove home the concepts in very a practical way that was immediately applicable for me."

— **LOLITA D. TONEY,** Community Leader and Senior Director of Development for the National Museum of African American Music

"This book is a 'Portable Mentor' for women at all stages of their career. It helps a reader recover quicker from the inevitable career pains and persevere towards the possibilities of your career when you stay the course. There is power in these pages and you'll find yours at the end of it."

— **CHRISTINA A. COLEMAN,** Private Client Strategy Executive

"What I love about Rita's book is how she encourages readers to 'own it' themselves rather the ubiquitous advice to 'find a mentor.' The latter too often is a crutch, a therapist, or way to abdicate responsibility. Phenomenal people usually find power within themselves and Rita tells how in an authentic and direct style."

— **JAN BABIAK,** Independent Board Member; Walgreens Boots Alliance Inc., Bank of Montreal, Euromoney Institutional Investors

TABLE OF CONTENTS

FOREWORD

I have had a front row seat to the lessons in this book for my entire life. Growing up as Rita Mitchell's daughter has given me both unique insight into why she wrote this book and unique access into the inner workings of corporate America. Frankly, it isn't easy to be a young woman in the corporate world—she knows this because she has been there, she has fought the battles you will face, and she has succeeded by any standard. Along the way, she has learned invaluable industry secrets to achieving success: secrets she has been sharing with me for my entire professional career. Now, she is sharing them with you. I can say without hesitation that the lessons contained in this book have changed my life and my career trajectory. Time and time again, I have been able to jump twenty steps ahead without having to bear twenty hard knocks.

- From being told in a meeting, "you aren't here to ask questions, you are just here to sit and look pretty," to being promoted into management three times faster than the norm.
- From lack of recognition by my superiors to being recognized as 40 Under 40 in my industry.
- From being told "we don't negotiate" during a new job offer to successfully negotiating an additional week of vacation and relocation expenses.

Still today, every time I hit a hurdle, I go back to the lessons in this guide and ask myself: What is the landscape/ environment that I'm dealing with? What is my personal agenda or endgame? What is in my power to change in order to get me closer to my goals? Then, I get my action plan together, go back to work the next day, and move my own personal mountains.

Despite all of the higher education, endless preparation, fine-tuned social skills, and unique opportunities I've been blessed with, I still could not navigate corporate America and achieve the success I desire without the guidance, direction, and clarity of this guide and the phenomenal woman who wrote it.

I call her the Oracle, and for good reason. To this day, even as a grown woman with a successful career, when I need help thinking through something, I call my mom and ask, "Is the Oracle available to chat?" When I get off the phone with her and go back into the real world with my new advice, it's like I have been given magic words or a secret code to success. She tells me to "blink twice, turn left, and click your heels," and, at first, I'm skeptical, and then I go, I blink twice, turn left, and click my heels, and BOOM! The world is my oyster. BOOM! I got promoted. BOOM! That person who was out to get me suddenly backed off. BOOM! I won an award. BOOM! I am now a keynote speaker at a major event. Magic, just magic.

Now, you, too, have access to this incredible knowledge, this incredible magic. This inspirational and entertaining guide will teach you how to quickly take the next best step in your specific situation, enabling you to go from point A to point B to PHENOMENAL!

This book was written specifically for you, to empower you to live a life that is truly phenomenal. It will show you that, no matter your background, experience, education, or credentials, you can have what you want out of life, and you can have it on your terms. Once you accept and own that you have value and purpose in this world, you can do anything: you can Own Your Phenomenal Self.

BRITTANY MITCHELL
SEPTEMBER 2018

INTRODUCTION

*O*wn Your Phenomenal Self is a comprehensive guide that represents a lifetime of learning, which you can digest in a short airplane flight or road trip. It is the essence of all I have learned in over thirty-nine years of success in both an entrepreneurial and corporate business environment. I believe that, when you read it, you will be empowered to take control of your journey as you travel toward your desired success.

By picking up this book, you are demonstrating that you are ambitious and highly motivated. I imagine, also, that you are early in your career, highly intelligent, skilled, multi-talented, and working in a corporate environment. You have a strong desire to do good in the world and do well for yourself and your family. You seek guidance from others in the industry who have attained the success, power, and decision-making rights you so desire, but perhaps you haven't been granted access. And despite all your best efforts and talents, you have been held back from promotions or other opportunities.

You need an unfiltered tap into the wisdom, resilience, and strategic prowess of a female leader-executive who has already fought the battles you currently face. You need to understand the three critical building blocks of character, success, and leadership that create the framework that allows you to do the real work of learning how to own your phenomenal self. And you need an experienced guide. *Own*

Your Phenomenal Self gives you access to an advanced level of corporate understanding and the career guidance you need to take control of your life and realize your destiny. Let's get started.

Character—
Finding Your True North

*True North is the internal compass that
guides you successfully through life.*

BILL GEORGE

Finding your True North is about establishing an orienting point for your destination. This orienting point is specific to what you want out of life and also to how you want to live your life. Once you decide and set your internal compass to your orienting point, nothing can stop you because no one person, no one thing, no one moment can take you off your path if you are determined to stay on it. Or, as I like to say, "One monkey don't stop no show."

What you need to know is that what is already inside you—what you have already been blessed with—is *phenomenal* and is *enough*, and, thus, your destination will be phenomenal; but you can't get to that phenomenal place without strong, unwavering character. When you remain grounded and hold firm to the character inside you, you will be empowered to step into your purpose and overcome the trials, tribulations, rejections, "No's," and funky monkeys that life will throw at you. And as you cross each milestone on your journey, that character will only grow and get stronger because character is a byproduct of the journey and the first building block to your phenomenal self.

The stories in Building Block I are about discovering and building the character that will take you through the ups and downs of your life and career. Whether it's understanding the importance of focus and determination in achieving your desired success, choosing to do the right thing for the right reason, or having the confidence to believe in yourself, these stories will help you set your internal compass, strengthen your character, and set you on the path to Building Block II: Success.

CHAPTER 1

One Monkey Don't Stop No Show

When you get into a tight place and everything goes against you, till it seems you cannot hold on for a minute longer, never give up then, for that is just the place and time that the tide will turn.

— HARRIET BEECHER STOWE

Over the course of my life and as far back as I can remember, I have been told by friends and family that "one monkey don't stop no show." Maybe because my family is from Deep South-Mississippi, maybe because I'm black, maybe because I grew up in a ghetto environment, or maybe because of a combination of the three—I'm not sure—I just know that this phrase was said often by people when things were plummeting downhill.

The phrase is even the title of several R&B songs about

love gone wrong, and in the African American community, it means that one setback should not impede progress. Over the years, it has taken on more and more meaning for me, and in fact, it has become one of my mental anchors, helping me keep both my psychological balance and the proper perspective in times of adversity. Just like the anchor on a ship is used to connect the ship to the floor of the sea so that the craft does not drift with the wind and the current, this phrase helps me to stay grounded so I don't drift from the understanding that I determine my destination and I control my destiny.

It might seem curious that a phrase about a monkey holds such meaning for me, but it takes me back to the first time I ever saw a monkey. I was at a Ringling Bros. Circus, and if you've ever been to one of these shows, you know how thrilling it can be for a young child: the lively music and swirling colors, the bright lights and unusual costumes, the exotic animals and the thousands of people—it is exciting and overwhelming at the same time.

The exotic animal acts were especially exciting to me: the elephants parading around the ring, the ringmaster putting his

I determine my destination and I control my destiny.

head in the lion's mouth, costumed ladies performing tricks atop galloping horses. But in all the animal acts, isn't there always one animal that won't cooperate? One poodle that refuses to dance, one tiger that won't jump through the hoop, one monkey that won't come out of its cage—that one funky monkey. When that uncooperative monkey stays in its cage, do the circus and the lights shut down? Do the music and the other animal acts stop? Do you lose your money and just go home?

No, of course not. Because one monkey does not, cannot, and will not shut down the circus. Because the show is much bigger and more important than one funky monkey. Because the show must go on.

You need to understand that, in your life and in your career, you are the show, and plenty of monkeys will come your way, some of which will try to stop your show. This is when you will have to decide who you are and what you are made of. It is totally up to you and in your control to choose how to handle it. You can shut down your show for that one funky monkey—the job, the promotion, the raise, the recognition, the credit, the supportive boss, all the things you think you deserve but do not have yet—or you can continue to move forward through adversity with sheer drive, focus, and determination to succeed and "go get it" despite that funky monkey.

Setting your internal compass is as much about who you are as where you're going, and it is essential to have a firm understanding of both if you want to succeed. Take stock of who you are. Determine your destination, maintain your focus, and let no one sway you. You may encounter naysayers and troublemakers along the way, but you are in charge of your destiny, and you get to choose how to get there. The decision is up to you; but for me, one monkey don't stop no show!

TAKEAWAYS:

1. One monkey CANNOT, DOES NOT, and WILL NOT shut down the show.

2. The show is much bigger and more important than the monkey.

3. You are the show, and you are in control!

CHAPTER 2

Stay Out of the Buffet Line

Govern thy life and thy thoughts as if the whole world were to see the one and read the other.

— THOMAS FULLER

My husband, Fulton Mitchell, was an educator and coach for over forty years, and in that time, he had the privilege of teaching thousands of children. Like many educators, he went beyond teaching class materials and taught important life lessons as well. One of the great life lessons he taught those children was the concept of staying out of the buffet line.

Being "in the buffet line" is likening the misbehaving students in a classroom to the choice of food items selected on a restaurant buffet. For example, in a classroom of thirty to sixty students, there is likely to be a group that misbehaves from time to time. And while it can be difficult to identify every disruptive child, Coach Mitchell could easily identify and punish the ringleader. In those cases, the singled-out child would always complain that he was not the "only one" misbehaving and that it was unfair to be punished when everyone else got a pass.

Coach Mitchell decided to teach the children to stand up to peer pressure and learn to choose independently of others. As he explained to the students, in the Physical Education Buffet Line, he was the customer in the restaurant, and misbehaving students were the menu items on the buffet line. As part of the "PE Buffet," Coach Mitchell could choose to pick one food item, several vegetables, or he could fill his plate with everything on the buffet. He could also decide to have one serving, or he could go back and fill his plate again. His plate, his choice; a little or a lot.

Coach Mitchell was able to get his point across to the children because the message was simple: actions have consequences, and if you make a bad choice, you run the risk of being on someone's menu.

This concept applies in the business world as well. You can expect that, at some point in your career, you are going to be tested and tempted to succumb to making questionable decisions. You will experience group peer pressure to succeed and win at all costs; you will be tempted to participate in office politics, which often circumvent the formal organizational structure; and you will also have your own ego issues as it relates to achieving self-importance. However, *you* have to make a decision to be accountable to *yourself* for all of *your* individual decisions and actions. If you are unprepared, you may find yourself flailing and making decisions that you most certainly will regret. You must set your moral compass now and be prepared to maintain it when temptations arise because all your choices will have some sort of consequence. You need to make the kind of choice that aligns with your ethics and your values.

Working in a corporate environment gives each person the opportunity to work in "gray space." This gray space is neither black nor white, but instead exists somewhere in the middle where you will have the choice to make questionable decisions and/or advance your career in a not-so straight and narrow fashion. These gray space decisions are the ones that make you hesitate and question whether they are right or wrong. These are the decisions that are right on the line. If they go your way, then you might get additional career acceleration, but if you get caught, you will be at risk in one way or another.

Set your moral compass now and be prepared to maintain it when temptations arise.

You will be tempted to categorize these gray decisions as not that bad, but these are the decisions that will land you in the buffet line. You must realize that there are consequences to succumbing to both individual peer pressure and to questionable group consensus, and these consequences can swing from minor to major to catastrophic. Every decision you make is important and stands alone. Are you willing to pay the price for succumbing to peer pressure? Are you willing to shoulder all the consequences of a group decision if you are the only one held accountable?

Choosing to operate in the gray space gives your boss the power to determine your consequences, which, ultimately, can get you off your determined course. You have to be careful, thoughtful, and wise in all of your decision-making and balance the desire for success with what you know is right and ethical because there is no such thing as doing a "little" wrong thing. Doing the wrong thing is like a cancer in the body: it grows and consumes what is healthy and good. Develop good character by making each decision as an individual who is doing the right thing for the right reason. Don't put yourself on your boss's menu—stay out of the buffet line!

TAKEAWAYS:

1. **Set and maintain your own moral-ethical compass and do not succumb to peer pressure.**
2. **There is no such thing as a "little" wrong thing.**
3. **Stay out of the gray space. Your performance, integrity, and metrics of success must and should stand alone.**

CHAPTER 3

Overcoming the "No's"

So often times it happens that we live our lives in chains and we never even know we have the key.

— EAGLES, LYRICS FROM *ALREADY GONE*

I am no stranger to hearing the word "No." Throughout my career, many people told me that the goals I had for myself were unrealistic and unreachable. I was told over and over by multiple employers that I was never going to reach my long-term goal of becoming an investment advisor. Wrong! I did. I was told that I would most certainly fail if I took the risk of changing careers or starting a business. Wrong! I did both.

Today, I am happy to declare that my goals were neither unrealistic nor unreachable, and all of the people who told me "No" were wrong. By seeing beyond the "No's," I stayed focused on my goals, chose my path, and owned my success. I doubled down, and I bet on me.

So, how do you overcome the "No's"?

DECIDE THAT YOU ARE THE ONLY ONE WHO GETS TO DETERMINE YOUR SUCCESS.

It's easy to become pigeonholed in a position you're good at, even if it's not the position you want. If you don't take control, step into the driver's seat, and develop your own agenda, you will most certainly end up in the back seat, riding down a road that others have chosen for you.

I was told over and over again that I should be happy with my role/job because I was adding value and delivering great results. Unfortunately, though my employer was satisfied with my level of success, I was not. It's up to you to determine your worth and value and to determine what success looks like for you. Own the work of the journey and you will have the end result that you desire.

GIVE YOUR BEST AT EVERY OPPORTUNITY.

Being successful means giving your all every day and having a mindset that failure is not an option. When I finally acquired the credentials to become an investment advisor, no one would hire me. Again, I received "No" after "No" after "No." At that point, there was nothing left to do but open my own insurance and investment firm, Mitchell Financial Inc., in my den. A new baby, bills to pay, and the hardships of starting a business out of the family house almost cost us our home. But failure? Not an option. Blinders on? Not an

Own the work of the journey and you will have the end result that you desire.

option. Failing to deliver my best effort each and every day? Not an option.

My husband and I worked hard through the uncertainty and built a very successful company. Another set of "No's" turned into more than a decade of success, proving that we all are in control of being our very best and owning our successes to come.

BECOME THE BEST AT YOUR CRAFT.

The skills required to succeed in your chosen field may not come naturally. The beauty of success, however, is that you don't need to be a natural at your craft—you just need to be determined to *become the best* at your craft.

Selling was hard for me at the beginning of my career. I had to study each and every part of the sales process: how to start a conversation, how to build rapport, how to uncover a need, and how to close the deal. Not a single part of the process came naturally to me.

Everything was difficult, and I could fill a book with the many "No's" I received as I developed my sales acumen. However, I read every book that I could get my hands on, attended every sales seminar that I could afford, and unmercifully picked the brain of every successful salesperson I met. I was determined to become a great salesperson, master the process, and become a top producer in my own right. I knew that, only when I mastered the sales process, would I be in the driver's seat to achieve my financial goals. It took everything

I had, but eventually, I became a top producer. What was previously uncomfortable had become natural.

DEVELOP "ALLIGATOR SKIN."

Somewhere along your personal and professional journey, you will be treated unfairly. The world is not perfect and people are not perfect. Know that it is going to happen. When it does, you have to remain focused, positive, and determined to stay the course to reach your goals. You will be told "No" all throughout your career. But, understand that you own the "Yes's," too; they are all in your pocket. Owning a "Yes" means that you and only you determine the next path on your journey. So when you hear a "No," put on your alligator skin, refocus, and take a "Yes" out of your pocket. You are in control!

TAKEAWAYS:

1. **Double down on yourself and decide that you are the only one to determine your success.**
2. **Give it your best at every opportunity.**
3. **Become the best at your craft.**
4. **Develop alligator skin.**

Success—
The Will to Win

Success is no accident. It is hard work,
perseverance, learning, studying, sacrifice,
and most of all, love of what you are doing
or learning to do.

PELE

Success is not an accident, it is a choice. You don't simply fall into success. Success involves setting a goal, creating a plan, executing the plan, and then winning with the plan. To do this, you have to have peripheral vision, a strategy, and a positive connection with people.

Ultimately, winning involves putting yourself on the line. And when you put yourself on the line, you open yourself up to failure. But at the end of the day, your desire to be successful has to be greater than your fear of failure.

Success both reveals and is predicated upon your character; thus, the stories in Building Block II follow from Building Block I. Here you will learn the importance of knowing the corporate landscape and strategizing in that context, competing and pushing yourself to be the best, and understanding the importance of interpersonal relationships and utilizing those connections. Once you master these concepts, you will be ready for Building Block III: Leadership.

CHAPTER 4

The Grass Is Green

Keep steadily before you the fact that all true success depends at last upon yourself.

— THEODORE T. HUNGER

The concept of "the grass is green" has been a guideline for me as a woman and as an African American trying to survive and thrive in corporate America. It has helped me deal with change, challenges, and opportunities throughout my entire career; and it entails understanding the corporate landscape and creating your career strategy based upon that landscape.

The premise is two-fold: the grass is green, except when it's not.

First, grass is green, and it grows green of its own accord. Even if I personally hated the color green and wanted to paint all of the grass orange, the painted orange grass would eventually die, and the new grass would naturally grow back as green.

I liken this to the gender and racial landscape in corporate America. It is there, it is tangible, and it is not going away. And in this landscape, it is naturally unfair and imbalanced as it relates to women. This means that, in a majority of corporate environments, you will not have the same growth opportunities; you will not be paid the same for your contributions; you will not have the same promotion opportunities; you will not be in the strategic huddle; and, yes, some of your great ideas will be stolen over the course of your career. This bias is even more pronounced for women of color. Unfortunately, this environment is where the vast majority of workers are most familiar and most comfortable. Again, the grass is green, and it naturally grows in as green.

You must understand the current corporate landscape. If you are prepared, you should not be surprised or shocked when unfair things happen. In fact, it should be the opposite. You should expect, anticipate, and be ready to respond appropriately.

This means that you have to work harder, be smarter, always be a great team player, and be more strategic because, every day, YOU are at a natural disadvantage in succeeding in this work environment. And because this work environment is comfortable to the majority, you are not going to have an army of people trying to change things because of its unfairness to you. I don't like it, and it's not sexy, but it is a fact. So, mentally, expect it and prepare for it.

Second, grass is green, except when it's not. When there

is drought, the grass turns brown. When there is a fire, the grass dies. Where there is pesticide, the grass does not grow. So, sometimes, the grass is not green, and, in fact, sometimes there might not even be grass. It does not happen often, but when it happens, the corporate environment falls out of equilibrium and the landscape changes accordingly.

Again, know the current landscape. When the grass is not green, there is unexpected opportunity for all who are prepared. In this moment, there is a very good chance that the corporation is in trouble and/or in transition; thus, the corporation is more concerned about the grass than maintaining the status quo of the gender or racial landscape.

For instance, the corporation could be in trouble because a strategy did not work; revenues are down and expenses are up; or unexpected changes occurred in management, legislation, the political scene, and so forth. When something like this happens, the grass is in trouble, the landscape has changed, and the corporation/manager/team wants to get back to that full, green grass as soon as possible. Frankly, when put in this position, they are open to any and all who are contributing, and the playing field is more even. In this moment, talent, experience, and proven results trump the status quo.

When the grass is not green, there is unexpected opportunity for all who are prepared.

Understand that this is not about throwing corporate America under the bus—no work environment is perfect because people aren't perfect. This is about figuring out the corporate landscape so you can get where you need to be. This is about you being in control of your destiny.

When the grass is green, you need to be sure you have an agenda, know what you want in a career path, and have a timeline to meet those goals. If you need more education, experience, or exposure, go get it, invest in anything that will separate you from the pack. Continue to develop your alligator skin and mentally prepare yourself to stay level-headed and strategic as you work toward your goals. And understand that you can only control what you can control: do your work, put your plan into motion, and continue to deliver an exceptional performance for your employer every day. If you do these things, expect that success will eventually come to you because, if you don't believe in yourself, no one else will.

When the grass is not green, be aware of it and realize that threats to the grass present opportunities for you. This is the time for you to be confident and step up as a leader. Be a problem-solver at the appropriate time and always come with a plan. Be prepared to build a case as to why you are the best person to lead, not just in conversation, but also in actual performance, metrics, and facts. This is not the time to be modest or shy—this is a time to raise your hand and claim the opportunity! And as before, by being prepared, you can expect that success will come to you.

TAKEAWAYS:

When the grass is green:

1. Have an agenda.
2. Get what you need to win.
3. Continue to develop your alligator skin.
4. Control what you can control.
5. Expect success.

When the grass is not green:

1. Be aware of the grass.
2. Be ready to step up as a leader.
3. Be prepared to build a case for yourself.
4. Claim the opportunity.
5. Expect success.

CHAPTER 5

Stretching Strengthens Your Core

One who gains strength by overcoming obstacles possesses the only strength which can overcome adversity.

— ALBERT SCHWEITZER

My daughter, Brittany, is a yoga enthusiast and is now practicing a new style of yoga called Buti Yoga. Buti Yoga combines dynamic yoga, plyometrics, and tribal dancing with deep core engagement. While one *could* choose to take a Buti Yoga class without any yoga experience, Brittany found that her many years of practicing more traditional styles of yoga, as well as her twenty plus years of dance experience, made it much easier to rise to the challenge of holding a downward dog position while isolating her glutes and "shaking her booty" at the same time. Unbelievable! It was those many years of building up both physical strength and mental stamina that allowed Brittany to quickly and easily embrace this new, vigorous style of workout.

Brittany was able to expand her physical capabilities because she had mastered a repertoire of basic poses that, on an ongoing basis, had caused her to stretch, which ultimately strengthened her core. This continuous work prepared Brittany to push her body to its limits, and it also gave her the confidence she needed to try new things and take calculated risks, knowing that, even if she initially failed, she had developed the skills to eventually succeed.

Strengthening your core is the key to success in most areas of your life, including your career. In this sense, your core is who you are, what you are about, and your strength of resolve. You must know and understand the core of who you are, and you must listen when the core of you speaks, because it will tell you when to stay and when it is time for change. Strengthening your inner core is critical to your long-term career success because it enables you to push yourself and take on risks associated with both challenges and opportunities.

Obviously, strengthening your core is an ongoing process, and it does not happen in a day. In fact, it will evolve throughout your career. In the beginning, it will involve stretching and expanding your thinking, your skills, your capacity for new challenges, your discipline, and your patience. So you must learn from the successes and struggles of people you want to be like and you must surround yourself with knowledge and information that guides, empowers, and inspires you. At this level, you will be mastering the basics, gaining confidence, and preparing yourself for more challenging work.

Later in your career, when you're deep in the trenches of the corporate world, strengthening your core equates to taking risks. You have mastered the basics, and success has given you confidence in your abilities and in your skillset, so you're ready to push yourself to meet challenges and to achieve even greater success.

At this level, you will discover that everything gets bigger—the challenges get bigger, the temptations get bigger, and the bullies get bigger. Without a strong core—without a strong resolve—you will not be ready to fight and win those battles.

Listen when the core of you speaks because it will tell you when to stay and when it is time for change.

On my journey to success, I had to make several decisions that all had a potential for loss. But each decision—each stretch—built upon the previous one and prepared me for greater risk and greater success.

FIRST STRETCH: Despite my success as a manager, I chose to leave corporate America in order to take control of my income and career. I accomplished this by becoming a successful salesperson in the insurance industry.

SECOND STRETCH: I chose to start my own company, Mitchell Financial, Inc., and work for myself when no one would allow me to work at the level of my proven success in either leadership and/or sales.

THIRD STRETCH: After creating a successful company

and becoming an accomplished investment advisor in my own right, I chose to go back to corporate America when I could *clearly see* both the opportunity for my skillset and the technological and regulatory challenges facing my small business.

FOURTH STRETCH: I became open to a new career path as a private banker, and I also became open to the idea of going back into corporate management.

FIFTH STRETCH: I chose to continue working for a company that had little regard for me or for transparency of communication regarding major decisions that directly impacted me and my department. This company also chose to empower my leader to make decisions around me, about me, and without me, despite my objections. However, I chose to stay on in my role as a leader because I loved helping people become financially independent; I loved leading and developing my team members to their desired success; I loved the ongoing challenge of creating new corporate strategies; and, finally, my compensation was meaningful to my family and my desired lifestyle. Therefore, I continued to support the company, the culture, and my leader, all while relentlessly delivering stellar results from all measurable company metrics.

MOST RECENT STRETCH: In order to continue my journey toward success and to achieve my personal goals, I chose to retire at sixty years old, leave corporate America, and put all of my energy into my passion of empowering women to own their phenomenal selves.

Risk-taking is the only way you get better, the only way your confidence gets built. Each stretch will build your confidence and each stretch will strengthen your core. And the stronger your core is, the greater your chance for phenomenal success becomes.

TAKEAWAYS:

1. Strengthening your core is a process and does not happen in a day; master the basics so that you can move forward stronger and with confidence.

2. Don't be afraid of new opportunities and challenges. Strengthening your core equates to taking risks.

3. Your core is who you are, what you are about, and your strength of resolve. Know and LISTEN to your inner core so you know when to stay and when it is time for change.

CHAPTER 6

Mastering the Connect

*Coming together is a beginning; keeping together is progress;
working together is success.*

— EDWARD EVERETT HALE

Phenomenal things and exceptional success are not accomplished in isolation; therefore, *you* cannot be phenomenal without connecting with others. You must learn to sincerely connect with people and become a master of the connect. And because people connect with those they like, know, and trust, it follows that you must be likable, you must know and be known to people on a personal level, and you must create a level of trust, which can only happen when you yourself are trustworthy.

At the heart of all of these characteristics is honesty, which according to Merriam-Webster is "straightforwardness of conduct." People can tell if you're fake, and they can also sense if you are sincere. Having a genuine interest in others and taking the time to get to know someone will go a long way toward earning trust and establishing a sincere connection. In all that you say and do, you must have integrity, a sense of caring, and you must deliver on what you say you will do when you say that you will do it.

If you work to develop these characteristics, then you will be able to exponentially increase the network of people who like, know, and trust you. This increase is necessary because, while having one or two people in your corner is great, it will not be enough to grow a career. And as you increase your personal network, you will simultaneously build your networking skills and grow your personal brand.

I started to understand the importance of connections when I worked at Prudential early in my career. Prudential had a very specific formula to teach people how to sell: the cold call. Every Monday night, we had to make cold calls from a phonebook; and the rule of thumb was to make seventy-five calls because, on average, seventy-five phone calls led to ten appointments, and ten appointments led to two sales.

Cold calling was not easy or fun. Every Monday from 6:00-9:00 p.m., when people were likely to be home from work, I would make cold calls. What I noticed over time was that the intensity of the call grew as I got closer to seventy-five. I did NOT want to make seventy-six calls, so I became more engaging and purposeful as it got down to the wire.

My ah-ha moment was when I realized that it wasn't

about seventy-five calls, it was about ten appointments, and, truly, it was about two sales. So, if I could get ten appointments out of ten calls, then I wouldn't have to make seventy-five calls. From that point on, I changed my mindset and adjusted my intensity and purposefulness.

Once I finally had sales, I determined that it was easier to get referrals from the two people who were now customers and friends than to go back to cold-call prison. That's when I learned to cultivate the relationship with each and every new customer so they all would be comfortable giving me referrals.

After asking them if they were happy with their service, I would ask if there was anyone they could recommend who might benefit from speaking with me about the product. They almost always said *no*, but when I asked about their hobbies or their involvement at church or a country club, it sparked conversation that turned into several referrals.

I knew I did not want to cold call **at all...ever**. I also knew that, in order to never have to cold call again, I had to master the connect before, during, and after the sale. This enabled me to create an exponential network of sales, and that is how I became a top producer.

Even today, when I go into a room full of strangers, I don't leave a room full of strangers. I introduce myself, I connect, I solidify the connection for the next meeting, and then I begin to build a bridge into their lives. Using this bridge, I can clearly see if I can help them succeed in their journey and if there is a need or benefit to them for what I'm selling. But I can't determine that until the bridge is built. Building this bridge connects me to them and them to me; I can see into their life and they can see into mine. And doing that with honesty, sincerity, and authenticity encourages people to trust me to tell them the truth, even when I don't end up selling them anything.

While you are busy building these bridges, it is also important to note that there are always six degrees of separation, or less, between everyone you meet. You have no idea who knows whom and who is connected to whom. You can't assume that, because someone doesn't look like you or dress like you, they don't have influence or power in a space that you are interested in now or that you might be interested in later.

You have to protect your brand and treat *all* people with care and kindness. There is a popular saying that goes: Be nice to those you meet on the way up because you will meet them on the way down. I believe that saying is true. Remember, you are building your brand for both the opportunities *and* the challenges you will encounter in your career, and the quality of your relationships will determine how successfully you navigate them. You can't do it alone. Master the connect.

> **Protect your brand and treat *all* people with care and kindness.**

TAKEAWAYS:

1. You cannot be phenomenal without connecting with others.

2. People connect with others they like, know, and trust; at the heart of this is honesty.

3. Create win-win scenarios with integrity as you connect.

4. Deliver on what you say you will do when you say you will do it.

Leadership— Casting Your Shadow

A leader is one who knows the way, goes the way, and shows the way.

JOHN C. MAXWELL

Leadership flows naturally from the attainment of success. When you reach success, it is clear to everyone around you that you own it because success happens in public. Success is loud, it's on stage, and people who are searching for it will want to know your secrets and shortcuts to success because they will want to emulate you. Eventually, you will have to decide whether you are going to help others attain success informally or in a formal leadership role. Whatever you decide, you will cast a leadership shadow because, when you are successful, it is highly visible.

The stories in Building Block III take you through the stages of leadership, from becoming a team player, to serving in the little things, to leadership excellence. All these stories reflect the fact that, in leadership, you cast a shadow. How far that shadow extends is up to you and the decisions you make. Nothing you do at this point can be taken lightly—your decisions make an impact on your career and on the careers of others. Being a phenomenal leader is within your grasp, and when you step into that role, you will be ready for the Real Work of owning your phenomenal self in the next section.

CHAPTER 7

Are You the Twelfth Player?

He who conquers others is strong;
he who conquers himself is mighty.

— LAO TZU

I have experienced many ah-ha moments on my journey to success. These moments have influenced my thoughts, my belief systems, and my work ethic, and they have come from a variety of places, including inspirational readings, great speakers, and incredible mentors. But perhaps the most impactful ah-ha moment came from my husband, Fulton Mitchell.

Coach Mitchell taught and coached thousands of children over the span of his career. In that time, I witnessed the impressive competitive skills, life lessons, and character transformation that can be taught and learned through sports. His concept of the Twelfth Player was especially transformational for me.

In his early years as a soccer coach, Coach Mitchell's teams lacked skill and experience, especially in comparison to the competition, whose rosters were often filled with travel players who had been playing from a young age. This meant that the competing team often had more talent sitting on the bench than he had on the actual field.

Coach needed to level the playing field and create a situation where his team had a chance to win. In effect, he needed more than the allowed eleven players on the field—he needed a twelfth player.

Essentially, Coach needed one player to act as two. That twelfth player had to cover two positions with the same skill level and intensity as two separate players could. That player needed stamina and had to be in tip-top shape and able to run. Additionally, that player had to be able to play both defense and offense and be innovative and creative on the field with the ability to see what Coach saw as the coach, while still being coachable. Finally, and most importantly, that player had to be a team player with a winning attitude.

If Coach could find or create that player, he knew his team had a real shot at winning. After some trial and error over the years, Coach successfully implemented the Twelfth Player strategy with great success in multiple sports.

The Twelfth Player concept completely changed my way of thinking. Although I knew what it meant to work hard and be the best at my craft personally, this concept made me think about my career and my leadership from a team perspective.

It forced me to think of success from a defensive and offensive position and from a winning and losing perspective. While I had made my mark as an individual superstar, how could I be a better contributor who made a difference for the team? Was I the twelfth player?

When I decided to become the twelfth player, it completely changed the way I thought about success and how I worked. This paradigm shift elevated my contribution to the success of the team, and it exponentially weighed into the performance of everyone around me.

In order for you to have exceptional success in the career that you desire, you must become the twelfth player on your team. You must be the player who makes a difference. You must be the one your coach wants and needs.

To become the twelfth player at your company, you must be self-motivated and always innovative in improving your skills and performance. You must show up ready! Ready to work, to compete, and to be a game changer. You must be determined to have success and have the mindset that "where there is a will, there is a way." You must put in great effort, have a great attitude, and set the bar for work expectations. And finally, you must be coachable and be a great team player.

You must be the player who makes a difference. You must be the one your coach wants and needs.

If this sounds like a lot of work, you're right! It is. But if you want to succeed in your chosen field, you have to be willing to work—and work hard—for it. Be a leader. Be the one your team needs. Be the Twelfth Player!

TAKEAWAYS:

1. **Work hard to inspire others by giving your best effort, having a great attitude, and delivering measurable results.**

2. **Be the player who makes a difference that both the "team" and "coach" need and want.**

3. **Become the twelfth player.**

CHAPTER 8

The Littlest Things Are the Biggest Things

The first responsibility of a leader is to define reality. The last is to say thank you. In between, the leader is a servant.

— MAX DEPREE

Over the course of my career, I have worked for and with many people, and I can honestly say that, when it comes to management and leadership, I have experienced the good, the bad, and the ugly. Most people think that good management is synonymous with great leadership, but that is just not true.

In my experience, I have found that most people in leadership positions don't lead, they manage. They manage processes, projects, budgets, sales, revenue, goals, and perception: they manage *things*. But in order to move people from point A to B to Z, you have to lead *people*—not just manage things.

Leadership is separate and distinct from management. Leadership is not being someone's boss and telling them what to think, what to do, and how and when to do it. Leadership is not using power because you have it and therefore you are powerful. Leadership is not trying to figure out how you can use your people to make you look great, get your next promotion, or leave your legacy. Leadership is setting an example so people want to be part of a team, mission, cause, movement, or journey.

Good leaders influence, empower, and inspire others to become the best they can be. Great leaders have humility and are, themselves, the greatest servants. They are powerful because they do the right thing for the right thing's sake. They bring out the best in others because they use their power and position for good. They help you to want to be your best, and they create an environment to nurture and foster that better behavior. With great leadership, there is care. With great leadership, the littlest things are the biggest things.

I have a friend who has mastered this concept. After a work meeting, he handed me a unique business card. It was small, only about one inch by three inches in size; but what struck me most was not the size, but what was on it. Along with his contact information, my friend's title was "CEO of Kindness."

It was amazing, and it stopped me in my tracks. I was both inspired and empowered because I realized that I, too, could be a CEO of Kindness! In that moment, I realized that the single most important thing you can do for someone is to be kind. To declare such a big message on the littlest of cards reflected not only great understanding but also great humility and service to mankind. That tiny card with the big message had inspired me to be a better person.

The following paragraphs outline several things I have learned over the course of my career. They seem simple, maybe even intuitive, but believe me, they are not always easy. Yet doing what is difficult is something that sets a good leader apart.

You must be honest in all your endeavors. Honesty speaks to character and integrity. Even when it is hard to be honest, it is always the best course of action. You cannot build meaningful, lasting relationships, garner success, and/or lead others without it. Dishonesty, obviously the lack of honesty and integrity, never ends well for you or others. Based on my life experiences, nothing dishonest stays hidden—the truth always finds a way to come forward. Honesty is, indeed, the best policy.

Honesty is, indeed, the best policy.

Your word must be your bond. As a leader, nothing substitutes for good character, truth, and trustworthiness. Always take the high road and treat others as you would like to be treated. It is not easy to do, but there will always be other opportunities to compete and to win when goodness and fairness are in play.

You must be kind and caring. I consider kindness to be king and caring to be queen, and they go hand in hand. People are inspired, motivated, and committed when you care about them and what they care about and all of your actions and decisions reflect the same. You must know where you are going. If it is a place of goodness, others will follow. And remember, greatness is not always good, but goodness is always great!

TAKEAWAYS:

1. **Honesty is always the best policy.**
2. **Always take the high road and treat others as you want to be treated.**
3. **Kindness is king and caring is queen.**

CHAPTER 9

Leaders Lead

A leader takes people where they want to go. A great leader takes people where they don't necessarily want to go, but ought to be.

— ROSALYNN CARTER

I believe that there are multiple types of leaders in the workplace: leaders who micromanage because they are afraid that no one is competent enough to do the job; leaders who are physically and mentally absent because they are incompetent, lazy, or both; leaders who have problems dealing with conflict and/or adversity, therefore they are afraid to make the tough decisions; leaders who lead from their personal playbook for the benefit of their own career (these are actually leaders who take); leaders with a combination of two or more of these stated characteristics; and, then, there are *leaders who lead*.

Leaders who lead understand that, with every decision they make, they cast a shadow. That shadow can clearly be seen by everyone around them, especially by the people whom they are leading; therefore, doing what is right, and doing it the right way, matters. Leaders who lead create and maintain a team culture where it is a win-win environment—a win for the company and a win for each team member—because this leader treats everyone with honesty, respect, and care as they create the plan to achieve company goals. Leaders who lead know that they do not have all the right answers, and they are not afraid of talent, smarter people, or collaboration. And leaders who lead embrace diversity because they understand that diversity makes the world better.

Leaders who lead influence, inspire, develop, and empower people to become their best selves. They motivate us to move from point A to point B to point Z—in thought, action, change, belief, and in purpose. Leaders don't just feed us fish when we are hungry; leaders also teach us how to fish so we can feed ourselves. Leaders know where they are going, why they are going, and why we should go.

Great leaders lead from a place of goodness. Great leaders not only lead others, but they also lead themselves. Great leaders know who they are and who they are not. Great leaders draw a "truth line" in the sand, which they do not cross. They stay true to their individual moral compass.

Leaders who lead influence, inspire, develop, and empower people to become their best selves.

I know several great leaders, but five, in particular, have significantly impacted my journey to my desired success. These four she-roes and one hero still impact and influence me today as I own my phenomenal self.

SHE-ROE #1
LINDA HAMSLEY: THE LIFE SAVER

I met Linda Hamsley at First American Bank, my first corporate job upon graduating from college. I was in the management training program rotating through different areas of the bank, and Linda was my retail rotation. She was the manager of one of the highest performing retail centers, and I worked as a teller for six weeks at her branch. Linda became my first legitimate mentor-champion. She taught me about banking, people, and sales. We would go to lunch often, and she would also take me on calls with her when appropriate.

Once I graduated from the program, I was promoted to an assistant branch manager at another location. By then, Linda had also been promoted and had moved on to additional leadership responsibilities within the bank. Becoming assistant branch manager was my first leadership role. In my new assignment, my boss at the time set out to fire me through documentation of my lack of knowledge and experience. His job, as a leader, should have been to teach me what I did not know; instead he only delivered meanness, continuous criticism, and treachery.

Linda stepped in behind the scenes and provided me the training and knowledge that I needed to succeed at the job;

but more importantly, she empowered and encouraged me to "tap into" her well of experiences whenever I needed her help or support. At the end of the day, Linda not only saved me from getting fired, she also created a place of trust for me to develop. She taught me that, as a woman, I had to "get ready, be ready, stay ready," and she showed me by example what a true leader looked liked. Linda not only threw me a life jacket when I was drowning, but Linda also taught me to how to swim without one.

SHE-ROE #2
DEBBIE CROWDER: THE CATALYST OF CHANGE

Debbie Crowder is currently Head of Branch and Premier Banking for SunTrust Bank, but I met her when she was the manager of the Medical Private Bank and I was the investment advisor who had been assigned to the private banking group for Middle Tennessee. I had an office at her branch and had helped turn around investment sales for her team of private bankers. I was part of her team, I was well liked and received, and we were having tremendous success, but Debbie saw more in me than just being good at investment advice.

Debbie thought that, in addition to selling and giving investment advice, I should also be leading. She encouraged me to put my name in the hat for a newly created leadership role for a new higher-end clientele. She believed I had the appropriate experience, the people skills, and the sales skill to be the new leader of this area.

Based on Debbie's advice and encouragement, I applied. Ultimately, I was not selected, but the process made me expand my thinking of the possibilities of what I could be doing with my career. Debbie made me think about not just having control of my money and my time, which had been my career drivers, but she also made me rethink my overall career trajectory. She did this knowing that, if I decided to do something different, she would lose me as a team member. But being the leader that she was and is, that was not the consideration.

Debbie was about inspiring, supporting, and empowering me to become my very best self rather than keeping me at the status quo for her own success. Through her leadership shadow, Debbie encouraged me to stretch and dream bigger.

SHE-ROE #3
MARGARET BEHM: THE CONTINUOUS WELL OF WISDOM

Margaret Behm, currently partner of Dodson Parker Behm & Capparella, is one of those women you want to know, talk to, and hang around just to be able to tap into her well of experience and knowledge. She has always been a trailblazer and an icon in both her personal success and in her ongoing generous acts that support women.

Margaret co-founded the first woman-led law firm in Nashville; she was one of the original founders of CABLE, the premier women's networking organization, which recently celebrated its fortieth anniversary; and she was the power and behind-the-scenes strategist for many women who went on to become the first women who were elected to their offices in Nashville.

I met Margaret through CABLE over thirty years ago, and she has become not only a mentor-champion to me but also a dear friend. Margaret, who is wickedly smart and is also generous with her time, helped me make many good decisions and also kept me from making some doozies, like the time I thought I might run for state office in my spare time.

She was there for me as I was building my business, Mitchell Financial, Inc., and also when I decided to go back to corporate America. She supported me by becoming a client, sending referrals, and insisting that I demand to be promoted to Senior Vice President, which happened; and later, she inspired me to push for an Executive Vice President designation, which also happened. She was even with me as I made my most recent career decision to leave my employer, retire early, write this book, and start a completely new chapter in my life.

Margaret has motivated me over the course of my career and has helped me move from point A to point B to point Z. She was one of the first women I looked up to when I started my business because she told me what I needed to hear rather than what I wanted to hear, and she is still that go-to leader for me today.

SHE-ROE #4
PATRICIA MATTHEW-JUAREZ:
THE CHEERLEADER

Patricia Matthew-Juarez, Ph.D., is currently Senior Vice President for Faculty Affairs and Development at Meharry Medical College, and, as a leader who leads, Pat treats everyone with honesty, respect, and care as they create the plan to achieve their individual goals. As stated earlier, leaders who lead know that they do not have all the right answers, and they are not afraid of talent, smarter people, or collaboration.

I met Pat when she first moved to Nashville from Los Angeles approximately fifteen years ago. She was referred to me as a possible client, and when we first met, there was an immediate connection. She instantly accepted me for who I was, and there was no hidden agenda. From that moment forward, Pat became the Rita Mitchell cheer-club leader.

I have never met a person outside of my immediate family who was so receiving of me, my goals, and my desire to do good in the world while still delivering stellar performance. Pat was the first person to tell me: "Rita, there is a book in you. You have wisdom, and it needs to be shared." She is family, she nurtures, and my successes are her successes. Her confidence in me made me more confident in myself. Her grace of sharing success and helping others to be successful was, and is, powerful.

Pat is a light in the darkness because she continuously brings care and kindness and selflessness to the table.

No jealousy, no ulterior motives. Pat leads from a place of goodness.

HERO #1
D. FULTON MITCHELL: THE PERSONAL AND PRIVATE TEACHER-COACH

Fulton, my husband for nearly forty years, is my soulmate and the love of my life. From a very young age (and to this day), he had a strong sense of self, knew who he was, where he wanted to go, and had a very strong moral compass.

When we married, Fulton was twenty-six and I was twenty-one; and from the beginning, he became my teacher-coach. A teacher teaches you fundamentals to be proficient at some skill and/or knowledge; a coach elevates you so you have the opportunity to become your best self. Fulton did, and does, both. Fulton always believed that I had enough to become successful at whatever I wanted to be, so he both pushed and supported me as I changed jobs, careers, and became an entrepreneur with absolutely no guarantee of financial success. Through his eyes, initially, and then with his ongoing support, I began to believe that I was enough, had enough, and could accomplish anything I set my mind to. And here we are.

Fulton is my teacher, my coach, my muse, and my best friend. The truth of the matter is that I would not be the person I am today if not for Fulton. Because of his kindness, care, and love, *I am who am*. I have made the hard choices and I have done the work. Fulton is my #1 hero because he is a leader who leads.

As a leader who leads, I believe there is a natural progression to becoming a leader. Leadership is built upon success, which is built upon character—you can't have a firm footing in one without the support of a strong foundation from the others. If you, too, want to be a leader who leads, you must follow this progression: you must learn from and work through each Building Block of Character, Success, and Leadership.

TAKEAWAYS:

1. **Treat people like you want to be treated—with honesty, respect, kindness, and care.**

2. **Do not be afraid of talented and smart people; embrace them. They will make everyone grow in character and all will become better.**

3. **Remember, as a leader, you cast a shadow with every decision you make, so know what you stand for, who you are, who you are not, where you are going, and hold firm to your truth line.**

Owning Your Phenomenal Self— Stepping into Your Purpose

I am here for a purpose and that purpose is to grow into a mountain, not to shrink to a grain of sand. Henceforth will I apply ALL my efforts to become the highest mountain of all and I will strain my potential until it cries for mercy.

— OG MANDINO

ongratulations on following through and investing in yourself! Your willingness to develop the Building Blocks of Character, Success, and Leadership means you are now prepared to step into your purpose and do the real work of owning your phenomenal self.

In these stories, you will learn that *you* were born and created a phenomenal being; that *you* are enough to accomplish anything that you set your mind to; that *you* own the power over yourself and your journey; and lastly, that **you have the ability** to do the work to own your phenomenal self.

This is the proving ground. This is the work! To truly own your phenomenal self, you must develop the mental stamina and fortitude to stay grounded in who you are no matter what the world is telling you, and you must build the strength and capacity to make the decisions that are right for you.

If you follow the guidelines in this book, you will find that there is nothing you can't accomplish. You are in control of yourself and your destiny. You can Own Your Phenomenal Self.

CHAPTER 10

Lights, Camera, Courage

Doubt whom you will, but never yourself.

— CHRISTIAN NESTELL BOVEE

As a member of the Tennessee Chapter of the International Women's Forum, I attend their annual retreats. One year during the opening icebreaker, we were asked to share a significant life moment. This moment had to have occurred before the age of eighteen, and the event had to be one that we remember as life-changing. As I paused to reflect on my first eighteen years of life, the visual that came to mind was my performance in my first school play, which took place in front of the entire student body, parents, and guests.

I was only eight years old and in the third grade, but I had auditioned and was ultimately selected to play the lead angel in the annual Christmas play. It was a big deal because, while there were several parts in the play, the most coveted was that of the lead angel.

To this day, I remember the moment when I was selected, as well as every detail thereafter. The teacher called my name, and I almost fainted. I was ecstatic and excited, but I also knew that it was going to be a huge amount of work to do my part perfectly. I practiced and practiced and then I practiced some more until it was finally the night of the play.

I vividly remember getting dressed before the play: it was the first time that my mom had ever let me wear my hair down with no braids or ponytails; I had a new red dress that had a can-can under the skirt, which made the skirt fan out all around me; I had a white angel cape and an angel halo hat on my head; and I felt like I was the most beautiful girl who ever existed. I was sure that this must be how Cinderella felt!

I remember arriving at school, going on stage, and waiting behind the curtains for my part to start. I was burning with excitement and anticipation and could hardly stand it. Finally, it was my cue. I stepped on stage, proud as I could be, and I said:

> *"Fear not; for, behold, I bring you good tidings of great joy, which shall be to all people. For unto you is born this day in the city of David a Savior, which is Christ the Lord. And this shall be a sign unto you; Ye shall find the babe wrapped in swaddling clothes, lying in a manger."*

I remember thinking, *this is what I was born to do*! In that moment, I was not nervous, nor was I afraid of making a mistake. I was beautiful, confident, received, and I was READY to deliver a perfect performance. And I did!

So why is this moment stuck in my head fifty years later? Because no one gets to stay in a perfect moment, no matter how wonderful, and no one gets a pass on the suffering required to grow into our best selves—the people we were created to become.

I believe that character is shaped and molded from all of life's experiences, but great character is developed through the fight of holding onto the goodness in yourself despite bad people, bad circumstances, and bad breaks. Over my many years of living, I have had many disappointments and less than perfect performances, including being bullied by the majority of the student body in both junior high and high school; being booed off two different stages—one by the junior high student body after delivering a speech when I was running for office, the other by the high school athletic student body when I received my tennis letter; and I was also threatened with physical violence by several school gangs on a daily basis in high school.

These were awful experiences, and they caused me to be less than confident. I was uncomfortable speaking on stage, my self-perception of whether I was going to be successful was shaken, and I was very apprehensive about trusting people. I had a lot of self-doubts about myself and the woman I would become.

However, in the lowest of these moments, in my most depressed state, that image of me at age eight, on stage in that red dress, always popped into my consciousness. I think this happened because, somehow, I knew that I was born and created a phenomenal being. I knew that, no matter what was happening to me, I had to get back to that person—the person I was before the world had an opinion. The person who was prepared to step onto the big stage at any time.

I had to decide that, despite how bad and afraid I felt on the inside, I would have the courage and the will to create my own grown-up reality about myself. My truth and my reality had to be the me who walked out on stage confident and fearless when I was only eight, where failure was not even a consideration.

Today, I am proud to say that, through much suffering, I have become a more humble, empathetic, stronger, and better person, and I am grateful for all of my life experiences. I overcame my extreme fear of public speaking to stand on the TEDx stage and deliver a talk on "Owning Your Power." Today I continue to stand and live in a place where I am strong, prepared, and always ready to step on anyone's stage.

What is that one moment in your life where you, too, were ready and strong?

So, what about you? Who were you before the world had an opinion? What is that one moment in your life where you, too, were ready and strong? Where you knew you were phenomenal? I know there is one, because we all have one.

But if you have forgotten that place, then make a place! Make a place where you see yourself as ready, strong, and prepared, and let that place be your anchor. Despite the personal struggles, hardships, and challenges, hold onto that place. And when you forget who you are, when you start to listen to the naysayers of the world instead of yourself, remember that you were born a phenomenal being and claim it!

TAKEAWAYS:

1. **You are who YOU decide to be.**
2. **Define YOUR life, don't let life define you.**
3. **Hold on to YOURSELF with confidence.**

CHAPTER 11

Grandma's Hands

Nothing is predestined: the obstacles of your past can become the gateways that lead to new beginnings.

— RALPH BLUM

My grandmother was tiny but mighty. Standing less than five feet tall and small in stature, Ethel Ernestine Lockett was a powerhouse, a "working machine," whose hands were all over my life.

She would wake between 4:00 and 5:00 a.m. every day, cook a hot breakfast for my grandfather, fix him a lunch to take to work, and then board the bus to go to work. She worked all day as a cook, a maid, and a seamstress for wealthy white families who lived on the beach in Gulfport, Mississippi, before taking the bus back home and cooking a hot dinner in the evening. In her spare time, she tended her garden, canned jellies and jams, and hosted the church youth group, the Sunshine Club.

She was religious, disciplined, and strict. Her life was not easy, but she was a woman of great faith, hard work, determination, love, service, and gratitude. She was a woman who served God, her husband, her family, and her church—in that order. I only saw her in the summers when we visited, but oh my gracious, how she helped to shape my life.

I realize, now, that my grandmother had her hands on me very early in my youth, and she was a tsunami force to be reckoned with. She was meek in manner, but she was loud and proud with her teachings to me and in her expectations of me. Nothing was hidden. She was honest, brave, God-fearing, and kind, but she was also a disciplinarian, and she boldly molded me out in the open. I always knew where I stood with her and where my place was in the world as a black female.

Recently, three major events revealed to me just how significant her influence was, how she molded my character and my value system, and how she helped form my determination to live an authentic life.

HIDDEN FIGURES

Hidden Figures is a movie about three African American women who were instrumental in and critical to the first successful US space mission to the moon. These three black women helped make it possible for John Glenn to orbit the earth and for the space crew to return home safely.

After seeing this important movie, the very idea that these extraordinary women and their amazing accomplishments were hidden and excluded from our history books was inconceivable to me. It made me pause and wonder what other historical facts had possibly been hidden; and it made me consider how the "not knowing" of a thing could both indirectly and directly shape the perception of African American people within our American culture.

As I contemplated these slights, my grandmother came to mind in full force. I thought, *these women were brilliant and so was she; their talents were hidden and so were hers.* I thought about the "not knowing" of facts and what could have been and what we might have had as a people or as a family had true history revealed itself, but I realized that, at the end of the day, they were all mute points.

Regardless of past wrongs, my grandmother's fortitude, her strong spirit of equity, her purpose, her determination for her children to survive, and, specifically, her desire for me to have success was not, and had not ever been, hidden. My grandmother had "loudly" put her truth inside of me as a child, and that truth was that *I was phenomenal.* That truth had been visible, tangible, and placed deep in my spirit even before I recognized it had been done. My grandmother affirmed that I had a purpose and I should keep it moving. What had been done was done, but I needed to be busy in the present and do the things that were yet to be done.

JOHN O'LEARY HALF-DAY SESSION

John O'Leary has an amazing story. At the age of nine, he accidentally set himself on fire and burned 100% of his body. He was given a one-percent chance to live. By all accounts, he should have died. Instead, he not only survived, but he thrived, learning to play the piano and write, in spite of the severe injuries to his hands and fingers. He now travels the world as a motivational speaker, sharing his passion for life and encouraging others to live inspired.

I recently attended one of John's half-day sessions, during which he instructed us to take a moment to reflect on the one person who had most influenced our character. He asked us to think about who helped us become the people we were today and if we were paying this influence forward. This was a very powerful moment for me because, to my surprise, the person who immediately came to mind was my grandmother.

In that moment, I realized that, from the very beginning, my grandmother had placed in me the expectation of "paying goodness forward" by demonstrating service, kindness, and respect to all in her own life: from her dedication to the church; to her running the church youth group, the Sunshine Club, from her house in the summer, where she led Bible study and fed us all very well; and to her teaching me to help the less fortunate because I was special and had been blessed with enough. My grandmother, in fact, taught me the Golden Rule: do unto others as you would have them do unto you.

2017 BLACK ENTERPRISE WOMEN OF POWER SUMMIT

I have never experienced anything like the 2017 Black Enterprise Women of Power Summit. In three days, over nine hundred powerful, influential, successful CEOs, executives, and affluent black women gathered to share their experiences and learn from the likes of Ursula Burns, chairman of Xerox; Marcia Ann Gillespie, former editor-in-chief of Ms. Magazine and Essence; Elaine Welteroth, editor-in-chief of Teen Vogue; and Bozoma Saint John, head of global consumer marketing for Apple Music and iTunes.

To hear their stories and witness their strength of character, leadership, vision, and determination was intoxicating, and as I was absorbing all of this information, another ah-ha moment hit me, smack dab in the middle of the conference: my grandmother had envisioned me here. My grandmother, who had cleaned houses and cooked for others, who had never experienced anything like this, had envisioned me being right here, right in the middle of phenomenal, successful black women leading. In that moment, I realized it was not my grandmother's vision, rather it was her *expectation*, and I was merely following through with what she had expected me to become. I walked away with a stronger sense of self and a renewed confidence that I could achieve anything I put my mind to.

All of the messages shared and received at these events only served to reinforce the lessons I had already learned standing at my grandmother's side as she cooked, cleaned, and worked hard for others. She taught me to be industrious and that success comes from hard work, discipline, and determination. She taught me the value of service before self and the absolute importance of paying forward the blessings we receive to others less fortunate. And, finally, my grandmother taught me scriptures, she taught me gratitude, she loved me unconditionally, and she believed unconditionally that there was greatness in me.

> My grandmother made it clear she expected great things from me, regardless of the circumstances, because I had been blessed with enough and I could overcome any obstacle.

At the end of the day, my grandmother made it clear she expected great things from me, regardless of the circumstances, because I had been blessed with enough and I could overcome any obstacle. Without me really being aware of it, my grandmother's example was a part of who I was then and is a part of who I am today.

Above all, she taught me that I am enough. You need to understand that you, too, are enough. Regardless of your origins or your history, you are enough.

Qualified, competent, and sufficient— you are more than enough!

TAKEAWAYS:

1. **Know you are enough and have enough to live your authentic life.**

2. **Have an attitude of gratitude and pay your blessings forward; the golden rule applies to all.**

3. **Work hard to achieve your goals, regardless of your circumstances. You are phenomenal.**

CHAPTER 12

Own Your Power

You are what your deep, driving desire is.
As your desire is, so is your will. As your will is, so is your deed.
As your deed is, so is your destiny.

— BRIHADARANYAKA UPANISHAD IV 4.5

After graduating from college and working for seven years in a corporate environment, I started my own insurance and securities brokerage firm: Mitchell Financial Inc. I was young, passionate, and driven to be a successful entrepreneur.

At the same time, I helped charter the Nashville Chapter of the National Association of Women Business Owners (NAWBO), and I volunteered my time to serve in my first significant leadership position on a well-established non-profit board. This nonprofit organization was created to help minority businesses gain access to corporate contracts. My role was to lead the minority businesses to do more business with large companies. In this capacity, I helped launch five big, bold initiatives for the organization, which increased our nonprofit's visibility in the greater community.

The work was very hard and time-consuming, which was significant considering that, at the time, my own personal firm had very limited resources. But my rationale was that, if I helped our member companies succeed, then my company, eventually, would reap the benefits.

I worked on these initiatives for a few years, during which I developed what I thought was a great friendship with the executive director. We worked closely and spent a lot of long hours on these projects. I believed we had developed mutual trust and respect for each other and that we were both working very hard to achieve the same goals. However, as the initiatives began to take off and each one gained traction, I discovered that this person was neither a good friend nor trustworthy. In fact, this person was a taker: a taker of ideas, a taker of resources, and a taker of perception.

This was a very hard lesson to learn, and I had to make some very difficult choices. I could either fight to continue to lead the initiatives I helped create, or I could walk away. I decided that the best choice for me was to resign from the board and walk away clean. It was disheartening, depressing, and embarrassing, but I knew in my heart that it was the right thing to do for my firm and for me.

Fortunately, a very seasoned, successful, female senior corporate executive, who had witnessed this entire series of events, pulled me to the side and gave me a piece of advice that had served her well in her career. She said:

> *"Rita, don't ever go into a meeting, take on a project, or enter into a service position without having your own personal agenda. When you don't have an agenda, not only will you lose your power, but you will also be serving someone else's agenda other than your own. This will happen whether you know it or not, so you should always be prepared for it to happen."*

This advice was pivotal as it introduced me to the concept of owning my personal power. When I had made decisions to serve in the past, I only considered the organization—its mission, its purpose as it related to me, and, ultimately, the value of my contribution. I had never considered there might be personal agendas on the table that were not in line with the organization's agenda or mine.

I asked myself: What is an agenda? What is power? I went to the dictionary. Merriam-Webster says that an agenda is a list or outline of things to be considered or done, and power is the control, authority, or influence over others.

Armed with the executive's advice and a new understanding of having an agenda and power, I stepped back and created my own personal agenda by asking myself the following questions:

- Who am I? What do I stand for?

- What do I want?
- Where am I going? Where do I want to end up?
- Why am I saying YES/NO?

The answers to those questions became my personal agenda—the things I valued most. And then, once I established my personal agenda, I had to figure out my power, or what I was giving away. I determined:

My Personal Agenda

1. To search for the truth and to do what is right
2. To support and help my family with all of my might, all that I am, and with all that I have
3. To serve like-minded people and like-minded organizations

My Power

1. My talents, my skills, my creativity, my knowledge
2. My time, my resources, my network, my professional brand

To this day, I filter everything I do and every decision I make through this agenda, and with every project, I evaluate my personal power and what I am giving away.

Before you embark on a new project, take a new job, or embrace a new opportunity, ask yourself: What is my personal agenda? Do I own my power? What is my personal filter? Am I in control of what I allow people to have and/or share?

Knowing the answers to these questions is essential to controlling your destiny and personal success because, if you don't know them, someone else may try to answer them for you. People may try to take your power and control you for their personal gain, and they may use trickery, peer pressure, and intimidation to do it.

By knowing your agenda and owning your power, you can be in control. You own your skills, your time, your knowledge and your resources. You get to choose how you share your power. Stay strong and focused on your personal agenda, and YOU will control your success!

Stay strong and focused on your personal agenda, and YOU will control your success!

TAKEAWAYS:

1. **Know what you stand for.**
2. **Know what you want.**
3. **Know why you're saying "Yes" and why you're saying "No."**
4. **Own your power.**

CHAPTER 13

There Is No Change Without Change!

The difference between a successful person and others is not a lack of strength, not a lack of knowledge, but rather a lack of will.

— VINCE LOMBARDI

What do you want to accomplish with your life? What do you want to accomplish with your career? What makes you happy? What kind of person do you want to be? What is on your bucket list?

The answers to these questions, which belong only to you, will not happen without embracing and owning change: change in your attitude; change in your work ethic; change in your expectation of what success looks like and what it takes to have it; change in your tolerance of what is normal; and change in the notion that others have power over your destiny. Because at the end of the day, if you do nothing different, then nothing different happens. There is no change without change, and YOU control that!

How do you think very successful people become successful? We know they do what others don't want to do, but it is much more than that. Successful people understand the "secret sauce": they know they have control over their lives and power over their destiny, and therefore, they must redefine themselves. In doing so, they turn themselves into the successful person they desire and hunger to be. THEY change. And if the environment they are currently in will not and does not support growth of character, redefinition, and career success, then they change that as well.

My first corporate job after graduating from college was with a local legacy bank where I was selected to participate in the bank's management training program. The premise of the program was twofold: be trained on the basics of banking and management, then complete a six-month rotation of working and experiencing major areas of the bank so we could choose where we wanted to be permanently placed.

The program was designed to last twelve to eighteen months, depending on the availability of the permanent assignment. My peers were all placed in the areas they selected, as promised after completing multiple rotations. I decided I wanted to be placed in the investment area, which was both exciting and mentally challenging. I was ecstatic to finally find the place I wanted to work.

Here is where everything became interesting. I was told that the bank felt I would be better served, and would ultimately have more career opportunity, in the retail channel. Hmmmm. That was interesting. I did not agree, but I had no choice in the matter. So, to retail, I went.

It was not easy. I was twenty-two years old, a recent college graduate, recently married, and was now promoted to assistant branch manager and a loan officer. In my new job, I was responsible for all branch operations and personnel, with the exception of my new boss, who was the branch manager. This created quite a predicament, considering the average age of the branch employees was forty; everyone was Caucasian; and all the employees were female, except for my boss, who was a white male and had tried and failed multiple times to be accepted into the bank's management training program, which I had just come from. What a nightmare.

Obviously, I was very excited about my new opportunity and promotion, and I naively assumed that my boss and the team would receive me and would want me to succeed if I did my part with a great attitude, enthusiasm for my new role and learning the job, exceptional work ethic (work early or stay late: whatever was needed), and eagerness to learn and grow. Dumb me.

What I did not realize at the time was that my boss and I had different agendas. My agenda: my success. His agenda:

to fire me for incompetence. This all came to a head when I discovered that his Executive Assistant was documenting my daily activities. She was in the middle of a customer phone call, and I was waiting behind her to ask her a question. The call was long, and while I was patiently waiting, I happened to look down at her writing pad on her desk. On the pad, I noticed that she had written a time sequence of events that started with the opening of the branch that morning: bathroom, 10:00 a.m. (5 minutes); phone call, 10:30 a.m. (10 minutes); lunch (45 minutes).

As I read the list, I began to realize that the activities she documented were the things I had done that day. To say that I was shocked and appalled is an understatement. I was infuriated! Of course, I immediately confronted her, then I marched into my boss's office and confronted him. He was stunned that they had been discovered; there was nothing left to do but own the truth.

My boss told me I was not worthy to have this opportunity and that I had taken this opportunity away from more qualified people, and that was why he was documenting me. He also told me that he was doing the bank a great service by uncovering my lack of competence and, in fact, that made him an exceptional employee.

I obviously disagreed with his perception and treatment of me. He was my leader and boss, and of course, I did not deserve this treatment. The question I had to ask myself was: What was I going to do about this? I needed and wanted to keep my job, so quitting was not an option; but, certainly, in order for me to survive this nightmare, something had to drastically change.

I realized that I needed immediate and serious help in coming up to speed; otherwise, I would definitely lose my job. I needed to figure out how to perform with excellence so there would be nothing to document.

Left with that conclusion, I called my first she-roe, Linda Hamsley (referenced in chapter nine, "Leaders Lead"). She immediately took control. She told me what to do and what to say, and she also told me what not to do. In addition, Linda created a space for me to learn everything about branch operations that I did not know. She made arrangements for me to come to her branch after I finished my work. She had been promoted, but the new manager owed Linda his promotion, so she enlisted his help for this task. He met me at his branch after I closed my branch, and he taught me how to be the best teller and how to balance my till, how to be exceptional at the note teller job, how to open and close the vault properly, and the list goes on.

This process went on for about six weeks, and by the time Linda got through with me, there was nothing that anyone could do to me. I knew everyone's job better than they did, and I could do their job better than they could. I was the best.

Here is the secret: because I HAD CHANGED, my work environment was forced to change. I went from failure to success because I made a choice to change. It was all up to me.

Within two years' time, my boss, who had tried to fire me, was demoted; the staff, who had hated me and had tried to

I went from failure to success because I made a choice to change. It was all up to me.

get me fired in order to support him, now loved me; and I had the power of both the performance review and the raise associated with it—and I used it. This power forced everyone to perform at a higher standard, which then allowed me to pay them at a higher standard. Additionally, the portfolio of customers at the branch grew, and they raved at our delivery of service.

I had done an exceptional job, and my performance review reflected the same. I had proven myself, and I felt I was finally in a position to begin looking for other career opportunities within the bank. In my naivety, I began to apply for available job openings. I posted; I interviewed. No offer.

At first, I thought I was just not a match, but as I continued to try to move from retail to other areas of the bank, I realized that the decision around my career had already been made by others. My career trajectory, the appropriate opportunities, my income, my potential, and my success had all been decided around me, about me, and without me.

In that moment, I realized there would be no change for me without *creating* change for myself. I needed to create a different career trajectory. No one else was going to do that for me. My ah-ha moment was realizing that, if I wanted something different, I would have to do something different. And

I did. I decided where I wanted to go and where I didn't, so I resigned. I took ownership of my journey and began a career in sales, which would become the cornerstone of my success.

So, let's end this chapter where we began: What do you want to accomplish with your life? What do you want to accomplish with your career? What makes you happy? What kind of person do you want to be? What is on your bucket list?

But before you answer, remember this truth: there is no change without change. What are you ready to change? What are you willing to change? What will you do next to make what you want out of life a reality?

My work is done. Your real work is still in process. So, what's next for you?

TAKEAWAYS:

1. **If you do nothing different, nothing different happens.**
2. **Understand the "secret sauce" and be willing to redefine yourself.**
3. **Know that you alone are in control of your success; take ownership of your journey.**

ACKNOWLEDGMENTS

There are so many people who have made this book possible. Thanks to my friends and colleagues who first told me I had a story to tell; and thanks to my professional team who helped me tell it.

I'm grateful to my editors, Nichole Riley-Doud, who worked with me through several revisions to make sure my stories were as strong as they could be, and Angelina Burkholder, who combed through the manuscript, making it sharper and clearer.

Special thanks go to Kristin Smith and Morgan Canclini-Mitchell, along with their entire marketing and publicity team, who believed in my message from the beginning. You kept me on task and worked tirelessly to make my dream a reality.

I'm thankful for Chris Ward, who captured my book's message and turned it into a beautiful cover.

Thanks also go to Mary Bernard, who helped me wade through the technical ins and outs of publishing.

My deepest gratitude goes to my family: to Fulton, my husband of thirty-nine years, whose love, wisdom, and encouragement are a part of every page of this book; and to Brittany, my daughter, the single most precious gift in my life.

Lastly, I am grateful for you, the reader, who will now be empowered to fully step into your passion and purpose and say YES to the ownership of your phenomenal self.

Made in United States
Orlando, FL
04 December 2021